Tiny House Living

Cardinal Rules for Ditching Your Clutter and Your Mortgage

Copyright 2016- Michael McCord - **All rights reserved.**

This document is geared towards providing exact and reliable information in regards to the topic and issue covered. The publication is sold with the idea that the publisher is not required to render accounting, officially permitted, or otherwise, qualified services. If advice is necessary, legal or professional, a practiced individual in the profession should be ordered.

- From a Declaration of Principles which was accepted and approved equally by a Committee of the American Bar Association and a Committee of Publishers and Associations.

In no way is it legal to reproduce, duplicate, or transmit any part of this document in either electronic means or in printed format. Recording of this publication is strictly prohibited and any storage of this document is not allowed unless with written permission from the publisher. All rights reserved.

The information provided herein is stated to be truthful and consistent, in that any liability, in terms of inattention or otherwise, by any usage or abuse of any policies, processes, or directions contained within is the solitary and utter responsibility of the recipient reader. Under no circumstances will any legal responsibility or blame be held against the publisher for any reparation, damages, or monetary loss due to the information herein, either directly or indirectly.

Respective authors own all copyrights not held by the publisher.

Table of Contents

Introduction 4

Chapter 1: Downsizing within Reason 6

Chapter 2: The Building Materials 13

Chapter 3: Off the Grid 17

Chapter 4: Parking your Tiny House 23

Chapter 6: Organizing Mistakes and Corrections 29

Chapter 7: Testing the Tiny 36

Conclusion 40

Introduction

Tiny house living is desired by many, but only a few pull it off for life. What seems wonderful during the planning and building stage can quickly turn against you, when you are living the "dream."

It seems magnificent when you are watching shows like "Tiny House Nation" and "Tiny House Living." People describe all the benefits, a few of the hiccups during building, and changes they had to make after living in their tiny house for a few months. But, the reality is often much different than what is shown on television.

Do you think a family of six is really still living in 100 square feet? No, when circumstances become better and life returns to affording a mortgaging for a full size home, you can guarantee the tiny house is up for sale.

If you do a search for tiny houses to buy, you will see quite a few, throughout the USA for sale. Often the captions read, "like new, lived in, but need to sell." In other words, for whatever reason going tiny didn't work for the owner. Several tiny homes have been converted to rentals because the owners no longer want to live in such small structures.

The question becomes—how can you be a part of the tiny house movement that is successful? How are you going to be the one that makes it work after spending $10,000 to $100,000 on your tiny house creation? It is by following some of the cardinal rules that make tiny house living a reasonable choice.

You have a lot to consider before you build your house if you want to become successful. The success factor comes in when you consider having no mortgage and decluttering your life to fit the "small" style you have chosen.

Learn how you can make your tiny house living arrangements successful from planning all the way through to living the "dream."

Chapter 1:
Downsizing within Reason

The greatest benefit of going tiny is gaining a mortgage free life. But, there are challenges to keeping your life free of any mortgage payment. The first challenge is "going tiny." Yes, it is a benefit, but it is also a challenge because you have to learn to live in a space that may be a quarter, a half, or three-quarters of the home size you are used to. There are certain rules that will make the choice to downsize easier.

The Right Size

Numerous studies have been conducted by experts on how much space the average American needs to feel comfortable in their home. These experts state that 100 sq. feet per person is the smallest amount of space the average person can live in. If you have four people in your family, you need at least 400 square feet for your home. Ideally, 500 square feet is better, so you have 100 sq. feet of community space.

Every person, no matter how close a family they are, needs time to themselves. It is not reasonable to expect that the great outdoors will always be able to provide you the space you need away from others. Freezing cold temperatures, where frostbite happens in seconds, if you go outside can hinder your "space." Temperatures in the 90s to 100s, or higher can lead to heat stroke. Thunderstorms with lightning, hurricanes, or tornadoes can also prevent you from going outside. Yes, these storms do not last, but what if you are cooped up for 3 days? Can you survive if you only have 10 sq. feet per person?

Most people find that sometimes there is such a thing as too tiny. The right size is all about knowing yourself first, and then knowing the other people you are going to live with, in your tiny home. If you are a married couple, with no plans for children in the next five years, then you may feel comfortable with only 200 sq. feet. But, what happens if birth control did not do its job, and you have a baby before you planned? Can you live in 200 sq. feet with a baby or for those five years before you can afford a larger home for your growing family?

The situations mentioned and questions asked do not mean you are going to answer the same way as the next person that reads this book. Rather, you are thinking about the "what ifs" and determining who you are as a person.

For example, one person interested in building a tiny house is comfortable living in a small amount of space, without anyone else living in that same space. However, this person knows that there is a need for high ceilings. An eight-foot-high ceiling is not enough, despite being just over 5 feet, eight feet high ceilings makes this person feel closed in. If there is not at least 4 to 5 feet of floor space running from the front to the back of the tiny house, without walls, the person also feels closed in. If you know things like this about yourself, then you can either plan to build a home that fits your quirks or you can immediately know that tiny house living is not for you.

Vehicle and Trailer Costs

The discussion on size must include the two options you have for building your tiny house: trailer or fixed home. A trailer can affect your downsizing benefits. Have you watched some of the tiny home shows on TV? Several people have built their home for $10,000 or $20,000 on trailers, but was the show specific? Did the show state the cost to build the house was $10,000 and this included the trailer? Most are ambiguous on this point. Typically, the shows are all about how much the materials, furniture, and labor costs were for building the house, but don't actually include the cost of the vehicle or trailer you need for towing your tiny house.

The next cardinal rule for reducing your monetary constraints is knowing what the vehicle and trailer will cost you in addition to the building materials.

Each vehicle and trailer has a GVWR or gross vehicle weight rating. It can also be called the GVM or gross vehicle mass. This is the safe operating weight/mass your vehicle can have. It includes the vehicle chassis, body, engine, engine fluids, fuel, accessories, driver, cargo, and passengers. For the trailers, it includes the chassis, axles, floor of the trailer, and all other trailer components.

Let's say you have a truck that says it has 6,200 pound GVWR, and the vehicle weighs 5,000 pounds. What do you think you can safely carry inside the vehicle? If you said 1,200 pounds, then you are correct. If you add a 300-pound tongue weight trailer, then the amount decreases to 900 pounds for the vehicle. So, including passengers and what you carry in the actual vehicle, you can carry 900 pounds, with a trailer.

The truck has to be able to tow the trailer size you want to have based on towing capacity and GVWR. Most ¾ ton or 1 ton trucks can pull the maximum trailer size for tiny homes.

Most states allow you to have up to 60 feet with a truck/trailer length. You may be able to drive an RV that is towing a vehicle and be up to 65 feet in length. For a trailer and motor home situation, which is the closest to a tiny house set up, you can be up to 45 feet in length, with a maximum height of 13 feet 6 inches.

Now, you understand the background information. It is time to discuss the costs. For a brand new 1-ton truck with a hemi and heavy duty rating, which is required for pulling the largest tiny house size, you would need to spend anywhere from $50,000 to $75,000 for the vehicle. If you are willing to fix up a used vehicle, you may be able to find an HD hemi 1-ton truck for $25,000 to $40,000.

Certain online tiny house retailers sell trailers for a maximum of $7,000, which is their 26-foot trailer. Other places may require up to $10,000 for a trailer that is set up for tiny house creations. You can also spend as little as $1,000 for a trailer, where you may need to spend a little more adding axles and welding the bolts to the trailer to secure the frame of your tiny house.

Let's say you are going for the larger tiny house, thus you need at least $50,000 for the newer vehicle and $7,000 for the 26-foot trailer. Already, you have spent $57,000 for the tiny house, without factoring in the building costs. Will this get you away from a mortgage or loan?

You might need an auto loan to fund your traveling tiny house, which may not bring you any further ahead financially. Remember that most auto loans are paid off in 5 years or less, thus your monthly car payment can be extremely large.

Now, if you already have a vehicle that can tow the trailer or already bought a trailer, these costs could ensure you get away from borrowing money from a bank. Everyone's situation is different. It is just a consideration you have to make when determining if you can stick with the cardinal rule of not having any type of loan at all to create your tiny house.

Land Costs

The thought that a tiny house is more affordable when it is not fixed to a piece of land can be somewhat of a myth depending on where you want to live. Obviously, some individuals want the mobility of a tiny house, but if you have no intentions of traveling then you may be better off finding a land deal.

Although rare, there are still some states in the USA that offer cheap land. It may not be in the most glamorous of locations, but if you work from home like many traveling tiny home owners—it may not matter where you live.

The downside is if you want to live in the city, such as New York, New Orleans, or other big cities, you may be right back to paying a mortgage for 200 sq. feet. Some tiny homes have sold for $250,000 to be in downtown New York, Charleston, or New Orleans.

There is one rule of owning land that can be appealing to tiny home owners. Land accrues equity, rather than depreciating like a vehicle and trailer. Land when it has a home on it, has more value. If you spend $50,000 on a piece of land and $10,000 to build your home, then you have at least $60,000 in value. The key, of course, is being able to find the right situation.

Land can also help you reduce current mortgage costs. You may not be entirely mortgage free for 10 years, but you would have a lower mortgage than if you purchased land with 2,000 square foot new construction built on it.

If you want to downsize to avoid high mortgages or any mortgage at all, then you will need to be savvy in your exploration for land. You could also approach friends or family that own land. You may be able to get 1 acre to build your home on for a reasonable value, if you know someone with land to spare.

An important rule is to go with what is most affordable as a means of avoiding the mortgage you ordinarily need for a home.

Avoid Expensive Tastes

Tiny houses do not have to be expensive, but they can certainly be unaffordable. One family built a tiny vacation home for $125,000. The home was around 200 square feet. This family wanted only the best in construction and technology. They wanted a tiny smart home, with a long granite countertop, wireless technology, and much more.

Your expensive tastes will increase the bill. This next rule asks you to think about what is most important to you, so you can avoid the mortgage or loan most homeowners end up with. It is also about making sure you do not blow the budget you have and spend more of your savings than you allot for the project.

If you want a full size fridge because you do not want to visit the store every two or three days, what are you willing to sacrifice in order to afford the appliance? When it comes to your bathroom vanity are you willing to spend $500 or can you make do with buying material for $60 and building your own vanity? To keep costs low and yourself mortgage free, you must be willing to compromise and sacrifice certain things you may desire.

Downsizing Steps

1. Determine your comfort level.

2. Examine your true self for space needs.

3. Do you need a land to accommodate your space requirements?

4. What is your budget?

5. Once steps 1 through 4 have answers, you may begin designing and planning for your tiny house.

Chapter 2:
The Building Materials

Keeping with the discussion of being mortgage free, and your tastes, we must discuss building materials in more detail. You are working out whether you can truly live tiny, not only in the affordability sector, but in other ways. Once you figure out how much space you need to live comfortably, whether land or a vehicle is more affordable or feasible, and that you must sacrifice some things you love, you are ready to determine how much your tastes really cost.

Granite vs. Butcher Block

Run a search on a lumber company website like Home Depot. How much is a piece of butcher block that is 8 feet (long) x 2 feet (width)? One store sells a block countertop that is 25 inches (wide) by 8 feet (long) x 1.5 inches (thick) for $159.00. If you search that same store, a piece of similar pre-fabricated granite countertop in white is $199.00. If you shop in stores that HGTV uses for their shows, then you should consider a granite countertop to be $50 to $100 per square foot. It also depends on the thickness of the granite and quality. The building materials you use determines whether or not you are spending $10,000 on building your home or ten times that amount.

Free vs. Paid

Many of the homes you see on TV had special supplies. People took the time to hunt around and find free barn wood that they restored and used to keep material costs low. Are you capable of doing the same? Do you have the time to spend hunting bargains, helping someone take down their barn for the free wood, or tearing apart pallets for the wood? It also has a lot to do with experience.

You may not have the experience to build without a contractor present. If that is the case, then you may not be able to save on the building materials as much as an experienced laborer who has access to free materials.

It would be nice if you can build your home for $10,000, but remember it all comes down to your tastes. Are you willing to sacrifice certain things like time, appliances, or granite countertops to be mortgage free? If you are, then you may be able to find many of the materials you need to build the house at a lower cost, ensuring that you won't need a mortgage to build your home.

Weight Determines Materials

Not only is the cost going to determine whether or not you have a mortgage, but the weight will play a part in certain choices you can make. This applies only as a rule to individuals who are going with a truck and trailer setup. You have to be cognizant of the gross vehicle weight rating for your truck and trailer. If you go for a granite countertop in your kitchen, the weight will be more than butcher block. One is wood and the other is rock, so it does matter. Your rule is to ensure the weight of your tiny house is within the appropriate maximum.

The benefit of this rule is that you will have to be less extravagant of decluttering your belongings further to account for the elegance of your tiny house on a trailer. The size and weight of belongings, such as clothing, books, computers, and other personal items you bring into the completed home, will determine the weight of the building materials.

Yes, when not moving, the gross vehicle weight rating is less important, on the other hand, if you have ten people in your home, with an axle that is already loaded to capacity with just yourself, then you are going to have issues.

Not having a mortgage is one extremely powerful benefit of going tiny, but if you want to survive tiny, then you also have to make allowances for the weight and thus the overall design of your tiny house. People do not succeed in going tiny, when they forget some of the very basic rules of building.

Engineers and architects are brought in on building projects because they have the expertise to ensure a structure is safe based on longevity and weather. A home in Colorado has to make allowances for heavy snow and ice weighing the roof down versus a home in North Carolina that needs to withstand hurricane winds.

You might save money on building materials, but can they truly get you down the road? Will your reclaimed barn wood withstand hurricane strength winds, when you are doing 70 miles an hour on the highway?

Going mortgage free is great, unless you sink money into a project that will be completely wasted after one trip on the highway.

It sounds negative. It makes going tiny seem really unappealing right now.

You should be asking yourself—is there a silver lining to the discussion?

Yes, remember the discussion about "knowing yourself," before you start your tiny house dream? The silver lining is based on your own perception.

Are you willing or capable of reducing your monthly expenses in order to get the tiny house of your dreams? You cannot be willing to sacrifice quality of building materials and overall construction because it will create safety concerns. However, when you follow the building material rules and suggestions, you can make a safe home, for a decent price, to avoid the mortgage you don't want to have anymore.

Building Material Steps

1. Determine the appliances, type of woods, countertops, and other building materials you like best.

2. Visit a lumber company or other location to price materials.

3. Once you have a list of things you want in your tiny home, speak with an engineer.

4. Have the engineer determine the weight of the materials based on their professional knowledge.

5. Modify your building material list based on cost and weight.

Chapter 3:
Off the Grid

You have a choice when you build a tiny house on a trailer. You can choose to be off the grid, unsupported by internet, TV, energy companies, and other utility companies. Living off the grid allows you to get away from the conventions of the world and live a simpler life. For some individuals this is a great option. For others, they like to be energy efficient, with certain creature comforts. There are ways you can make tiny house living more comfortable for you, while reducing certain amounts of clutter. It is going to depend on the amount of money you wish to use to build your tiny home. The motto is to keep away from mortgages and loans, which could limit your desire to build a more energy efficient home that is semi or completely off grid.

Solar Power

Your home size will determine the number of solar panels you will need to live off grid. For a solar power system, you require solar panels, a controller, battery, and inverter. The battery is going to accept the charge from the sun, while the inverter will convert the battery energy into usable electricity in the home. Good batteries for a solar array can run upwards of $400 or you can purchase batteries like those for a car, but you are going to replace those more often. You can purchase solar panel kits that offer 400 watts for under $1500. Other systems offer more wattage based on the number of panels and can run upwards of $20,000 depending on the system and the panels you purchase. Of course, there are definite savings after the fact.

First, you will not need to find a location that supplies you with an electrical hookup. Boondocking becomes more of an option, when you don't have to consider finding a power source.

If you are not mobile, then you do not have to sign up and pay for any energy company to supply you with electricity. You save because you are no longer paying out a high monthly bill or any bill at all.

The initial cost may be higher, but the overall savings and lower carbon footprint make solar power the best option for tiny houses.

To figure out the number of solar panels you need, you have to know the draw of your electrical devices. Do not forget any electrical device you might be using, if only sometimes plugged in. It will all matter.

Here are common devices you might have:

- Laptop
- Tablet
- Smartphone
- Fridge/freezer
- Washer/dryer
- Stove
- Coffee maker
- Toaster

- Mixer
- Light fixtures
- TV
- Hair dryer
- Curling iron

Anything you plug in is going to draw on the solar energy. How much it draws depends on how long it is plugged in, whether it needs to run like a fridge to keep cool, or if you can use the battery for a few days before you need to plug in the device again. Obviously, the fewer items you keep plugged in throughout the day, the less you are going to draw on your energy.

Propane

Propane also needs to be figured, when designing your tiny house. A propane tank will take some weight consideration, as well as how much you need to carry before you need to get a refill. If you are using any propane hot water heater, or gas appliances, then you may need more than a regular sized tank. You might need two propane tanks. Another thing to consider, in order to make your tiny living successful, is how easy will it be to switch out the propane tank or tanks? If you are in the middle of the desert for three weeks, where civilization is 100 miles away will you have enough propane?

It is the little things that can make traveling more difficult in a tiny home. When space is at a minimum and you don't have basic necessities, it is possible for tempers to flare. One way to avoid this and be happy in your tiny house living is to plan correctly for the situations you are going to be in.

Water Tank

Water is a similar discussion to propane. You need to know you have enough clean water for the basic necessities, but also be cognizant of the weight. For water tanks, you have a clean tank and a gray water tank. Anytime you shower, wash your hands, or wash dishes, you are going to have gray water (dirty water). This water has to be disposed of at proper locations because of the soap and other chemicals that are in the water. You have to plan to have enough water on board to avoid running out when you need it most. A 400-gallon water tank is not small and it is very heavy when filled with water. A family of four may require such a tank, with a fill up every other day. One person may be able to drive around with 200 gallons in their water tank for a week before needing to fill up the water tank. It depends on the number of showers, cooking, and other uses you have for water. The rule is to think about it, determine the size of tank needed, and factor this into your plan as a means of determining whether you should declutter other aspects of your life to fit an important need—water.

Other Utilities

In a day and age where computers, tablets, and smartphones are everything in our existence, you may feel you want to be on the grid just a little for certain utilities such as TV and internet. But, is it possible with a mobile tiny house? Can you find a cost effective way to stay hooked into the media?

The short answer is yes, but the longer answer is that it all depends on you. What do you use your internet for? How often do you watch TV? Are you more likely to stream an entire season or do you have to watch the show when it first airs? If you work and travel, then how often are you on your computer using data?

For example, if you stream internet TV for 4 hours a day, spend 8 hours surfing the net doing research, and sending 100s of emails a dongle from Verizon or any other mobile phone service provider is not going to provide sufficient data for your internet needs. Companies like Comcast and Century Link are land based.

This leaves you with satellite internet and TV. A lot has occurred in five years, where you can now find better satellite internet packages, although they are more expensive than land based companies. It does give you the option of staying hooked in to the online world. TV is as simple as choosing which satellite provider you like best and then directing the satellite in the right direction based on where you have stopped for the time being.

Off the Grid Steps

1. Ascertain if solar power is within your budget.
2. Use online websites to determine the draw of your appliances.
3. Use the information from step 2 to buy the solar panel package required.
4. Determine what appliances use propane.
5. Assess how much propane is required for standard operation.

6. Buy the needed tanks.

7. Calculating the weight of water.

8. Purchase clean water tanks and gray water tanks based on the weight of water.

9. Request price quotes from utility companies for TV and internet, if you wish to be semi-off the grid.

Chapter 4:
Parking your Tiny House

Another challenge you will face is where to park your tiny house. Your goal is to be mortgage free, with less clutter in your home. However, what is going to happen when you need a place to park your mobile tiny house? Will you be able to find a location? Will your tiny house be welcome? Unfortunately, there are more and more restrictions each year, when it comes to parking your tiny house in certain locations.

Tiny House Communities

Certain cities around the USA are starting tiny house communities. Lyons, Colorado and Portland, Oregon are two places that have tiny house communities. Some RV parks in California have allowed tiny house constructions.

Your challenge is to ask whether some of these communities are safe. Are they a place you would want to raise children? Like RV parks and manufactured home communities, you are going to have all varieties of people living in the area. You will want to do your due diligence to ensure you are choosing a safe place to park, while traveling.

Not all communities are going to be "free" parking. You may discover that the fees are just as high as RV parks. Rental fees will be discussed later on in more detail.

RV Park

In the last year or two, RV parks have been changing their mind as to whether you can park your tiny house. As with many mainstream communities, people living in RV parks are deciding that tiny houses are not uniform to RVs and are too individual or too oversized to be in an RV park. Perhaps, it is more that RV parks are hard to come by that are affordable and RV travelers do not want their spaces taken up. Unless you ask at each location, the reason you may be turned away will remain unclear. It is known that RV parks are certainly getting stricter. It makes it difficult to find locations to park, outside of land friends and family may allow you to occupy when you are in the vicinity.

Boondocking

Boondocking is an RV term, used to describe staying on someone else's land or finding "free" land. Public land that does not require a fee for a camping location, but permits camping, is a great way to travel. Unfortunately, in the USA there are few boondocking locations available. The locations that are available are usually privately held, but provided to you for trade or a small fee. There are boondocking forums and websites, where you can locate places to stay.

Rent

Public locations that offer campsites, RV sites, or parking for tiny houses usually have site rental fees. These fees can be as much as a mortgage. Some locations charge more than $700 for you to park for a month.

It does not put you any further ahead to pay a high fee for spot rental, for a month, if you are paying the same amount for the site rental as you would for a mortgage on a $150,000 valued house.

Again, it does seem negative, when you read this information. But, do not get discouraged. There are certain people and communities, making tiny house living possible. The challenge is doing your research and finding locations to park, based on your travel desires. You have to go into tiny house living with your eyes open. The cardinal rule for this chapter is that you cannot assume you will always be able to find a place to park. RVs can usually get away with parking in truck stops or certain retail store parking lots, but a tiny house is more noticeable. You have to seek permission for parking when the land is owned by another. Just keep in mind that your research is paramount to making tiny house living a success based on your travel patterns.

Parking your Tiny House Steps

1. Plan your current trip.
2. Purchase subscriptions to AAA, boondocking websites, and RV parks.
3. Search for tiny house communities along the route.
4. Assess the possible locations for parking on your trip route.
5. Call ahead for availability and booking requirements.
6. Set up parking options along the route before you leave on your trip.
7. **Chapter 5: Decluttering and Guilt**

Part of successful tiny house living is based on the functionality of your home. So far the discussion has been in how to reduce the need for a mortgage or how to live without spending a great deal on your tiny house life. Now, you will want to focus on the comfort of your home. The items you are able to bring into your tiny home are based on space, weight, and functionality.

A person with a stationary tiny home does not have to worry about weight, but you will need to be concerned with space and functionality. There are innovative organization methods, but "know yourself." Are you the type of person who will put away things after you have used them or do you let things pile up? Are you truly a person who can make your bed every day, when the necessity is there or will you avoid such a chore?

Living in a tiny house requires a hyper-organized and a proactive nature. If you cannot keep your space clean now, how likely will you be able to do so if you bring in a lot of things?

There are definitely rules you must follow to declutter your life for going tiny, as well as to ensure you do not feel guilty when you get rid of something.

Decluttering Rules

1. If you have not used the item within the last six months, it goes.

2. Any duplicates of books, photos, or other items, you keep one.

3. Take photos of nostalgic keepsakes, then donate or sell them.

4. If you don't like it, and it was a present, it goes.

5. Find a home for all items or design your house to have a place for all items.

6. Start putting things away now, before your tiny house is built. Practice keeps you in an appropriate routine.

7. Think "someone else needs this more than I do." It helps you eliminate things you no longer use, and cannot take with you into your tiny home.

8. If you wouldn't buy the item today, it goes. If an item no longer fits into your décor, home size, or preferences, do not keep it.

9. Examine your spending habits. Do you truly need something that will add to your tiny house clutter?

10. Follow the rules and keep repeating them until you can eliminate all but the essential items.

Getting Rid of the Guilt Rules

1. Do you truly like an item you own that someone gave you?

2. Is the heirloom something you treasure because you find it attractive?

3. Have you ever given a gift that wasn't right, and wished the person would donate it or return it to the store?

If you have an item that someone gave you and you like it, keep it, if it is something you can fit into your tiny house. If the gift is unlikable because it is not your style or you find it ugly, remember, "It is your life!" Sometimes gift giving goes wrong. You cannot let the guilt weigh you down.

A coworker brought back soap from their month long trip. The person who received the gift is allergic to perfume. Should that person suffer the allergic reaction, and keep the soap? No. Should they feel guilty about giving it to someone else or getting rid of it? Of course, not. They also shouldn't make the gift giver feel guilty by not accepting the gift and giving a solid reason as to why.

You have honest justifications for getting rid of gifts others have given you, for taking pictures of heirlooms or passing them on to other family, as well as understanding that you too have given wrong gifts.

As long as you can accept the truth that not all things can be liked or enjoyed, you can donate, sell or trash items you do not need, want, or cannot fit into your tiny home lifestyle.

Chapter 6:
Organizing Mistakes and Corrections

One of the most difficult parts of living tiny is having enough organization and space for the items you wish to bring. Many tiny house owners have added storage or removed built in options in order to gain more organization and storage. It is costly to remove things after you have built them, not only money wise, but also time wise. You purchased the materials, drew up the plans, and then you have to go in and modify everything. There are ways you can avoid these costly mistakes by following certain rules.

Tape off the House Design

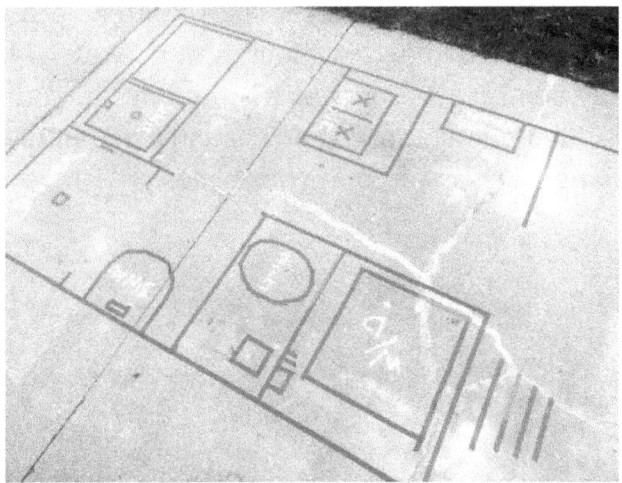

1. You will need to visit an architect to draw up house plans for you, unless you are capable of designing the house.

2. From the plans, tape or draw out the layout with proper measurements, either outside or inside your current home.

3. Include all areas you will have for storage.

4. Begin by bringing in the items that are most important.

5. Place these items in your design in the areas of storage you have.

6. Since the layout is not 3-D, you are going to have to use a tape measure to ensure you are not stacking your items too high for the storage space you have. For example, in floor storage in a loft, is only as high as the joists you are using between the ceiling and the floor.

By laying out the design and testing the area with the items you have, you will know whether or not you have enough storage for the organization you wish to have in your home. It also helps you understand just how small tiny can be. You may end up changing the plan to fit your needs.

Bear in mind you also have vertical space.

You can use the walls for some storage, but not for everything. As you layout your design, think about what you can put on the walls.

Clothing Issues

Clothing is one of the biggest issues tiny house owners have. How can they bring along the clothing they need for work, dinner parties, and other events? For some clothing is less important. One person may be happy with one outfit for every occasion, as long as they have five days of work outfits or uniforms. There have been other individuals that required a full walk in closet, which was possible based on innovative designs by professionals. Your clothing issue can be all about innovative concepts, such as how to hang your numerous scarves.

You can use shower curtain rings to hang scarfs on a single hanger. Another person used a circular tie rack to accomplish the same thing. The key will be to test the appropriate closet space for the items you own, as well as to look around at different locations.

1. Visit places like Ikea, which are known for their tiny room setups with closet space.

2. Take time to go to closet stores to see what they offer in terms of design.

3. Speak with a designer.

You can always visit stores and speak with designers for free. You can take the ideas you see or are given and implement them into your tiny house.

4. Lay out your closet space, either in the closet you have now or by using tape to simulate the closet.

5. How functional is the space?

6. Can you fit everything you need?

If you can answer positively to steps 5 and 6, then you know the closet is going to work for you in your tiny house. If it is not functional and you cannot include all your clothing and shoe needs, go back to the drawing board.

Additions

Yes, additions or changes to your home are more expensive than getting it right the first time. However, there are some things that no matter how much time you give to plan for them that do not turn out as you hoped. Some tiny house owners have had to do the following:

1. Live in the house for a month.

2. Keep everything how it was the day they moved in.

3. Make changes after a month by adding more storage, removing certain furniture pieces, or building in others.

There are ways to avoid this issue. As you read in the other two organization sections, you can lay out your tiny house and test how functional it will be before you move in. There is no guarantee that it will work, but it is certainly an option.

Another step is to conduct research before you leave the planning stage.

1. Visit online storage sites.

2. Search Pinterest for storage ideas.

3. Go to tiny house forums.

4. Go to storage forums.

The more information you have, the easier it will be to create a tiny house that will work for you. Sometimes an internet search cannot be avoided. It is common sense, but you also have to know how to search.

Are you going to get ideas simply by typing in storage? Probably not. The keywords you use will help direct you towards the answers.

For instance, "tiny house storage hacks" brings up 1000 ideas on Pinterest. You will see ways to make extra storage, but not all of these ideas are going to be the correct option.

Case and point: storage between the studs.

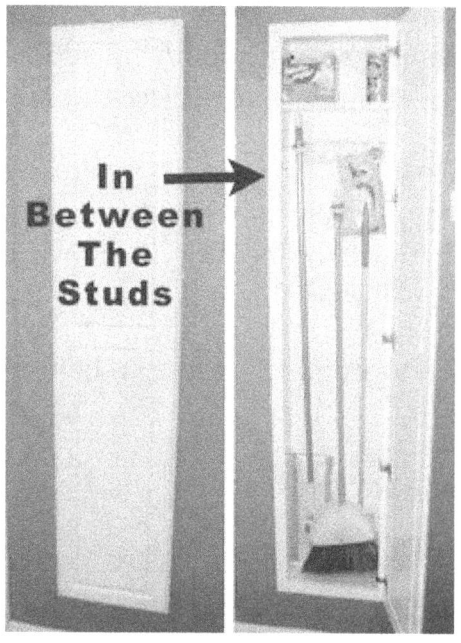

There is a flaw in this concept if you do not create the storage space correctly. This person bought a cabinet to prevent issues with insulation. When you leave a wall open, you have no insulation in that wall space. It can lead to inefficiency with your heating system. With a cabinet you are at least plugging any potential air leaks by using trim. Also between the cabinet and the studs, you still use a thin layer of insulation. If you just build shelves in the space, without proper insulation, then you are losing heat in winter or allowing hot air in during the warmer months.

Innovations exist and you may have a mind to come up with ideas all on your own. Just make certain you are not breaking the cardinal rule of this chapter: **test out the organizing ideas in a comparable space before you build it in a tiny house.**

Chapter 7:
Testing the Tiny

During the planning stage you are going to test the tiny house concept in all manner of ways. In recent chapters, the focus was on laying out the tiny house space with tape. In this chapter, you are going to find other steps to testing out the tiny for the success of living in your tiny house.

Rent a Tiny House

Remember the mention that some people are selling their tiny homes because they could not make it a success. Others who are no longer living in their tiny homes are renting them out. There is a whole online community where you can search for tiny house rentals from 96 sq. feet up to 1,000 sq. feet. You have the option of testing whether or not you could live in a tiny house with another person or your entire family.

It is imperative that you do so.

1. Search online for tiny house rentals.
2. Find a comparable tiny house based on the square footage design you are contemplating.
3. Rent the home for at least a week, but a month would be better.
4. Stay in the house with only the essentials.
5. Get a feel for how you need to adapt your life to fit in a tiny space.

At the end of the test, you may need to go back to your plan and modify it for more space, extra storage, or other changes.

Block Out Similar Space in Your Home

If you are unable to rent a tiny house due to the expense, then use the place you currently live in. This is where the tape will come in handy again.

1. Layout only enough space in each area of your home that you will have in your tiny house.

2. For the bathroom, tape off the sink, toilet, and shower area based on the square footage that will be inside your tiny home.

3. Do the same for each room, ensuring that you are not going over the "line" of space.

4. Rearrange the space you have taped off, so that what you need is within the lines.

5. Live this way, for two months.

Did you survive the test? Did you go over the line? Have you gone back to your tiny house plan to change certain parameters to make it easier to live in a tiny space? It is okay to answer yes, you had to modify your plan.

It is better to know that you are able to live tiny in the space you have because you have made a success of it already.

Conduct Tests with your Partner

For these tests, you do not need to tape off everything, but you do have to see how it will be to live tiny. It is not only about the space you will have, but the communication.

1. Start with the kitchen.

2. Set up an area of space that is comparable to the tiny house you are planning.

3. With your partner make a meal only in that space.

4. Again, bring only what you will have in the tiny house in that space.

5. See how you move with each other.

Did someone fall out of the space? Did you elbow your partner in the face, ribs, or step on their toes? Did you find you need to communicate better?

When you live in a tiny house, communication is key. While you are testing the tiny as the cardinal rule of planning, remember that open, voiced communication is the cardinal rule of living tiny.

If you have problems communicating now because you think the other person is just going to know what you want, then you need to work on your communication.

1. Start by being more vocal.

2. Do not assume the other person knows what you need or want.

3. Count to ten when you feel anger and try to communicate again.

4. Slow down. Your pace in life needs to be slower when you live tiny, to ensure you are thinking, listening, and communicating correctly.

5. Seek a communication class if you find you are still having issues.

Conclusion

Living tiny requires changes within yourself. If there is one cardinal rule you take away from this book—it should be that you need to know yourself better.

Until you can sit in front of another and tell them who you are, what your strengths and weaknesses are, and be open about your personality, without worry of criticism, going tiny will be difficult.

It comes down to being honest with yourself about what you can and cannot stand. If you don't know your weaknesses or do not like criticism, then when you live in a tiny house with another person, you won't have the open communication you need for your life to be successful.

All the rules in the world about how to downsize, use proper building materials, go off grid, parking your tiny house, decluttering, organizing, and testing the tiny will not work if you do not know who you are, your limits, and gain better communication.

www.ingramcontent.com/pod-product-compliance
Lightning Source LLC
Chambersburg PA
CBHW070421190526

45169CB00003B/1355